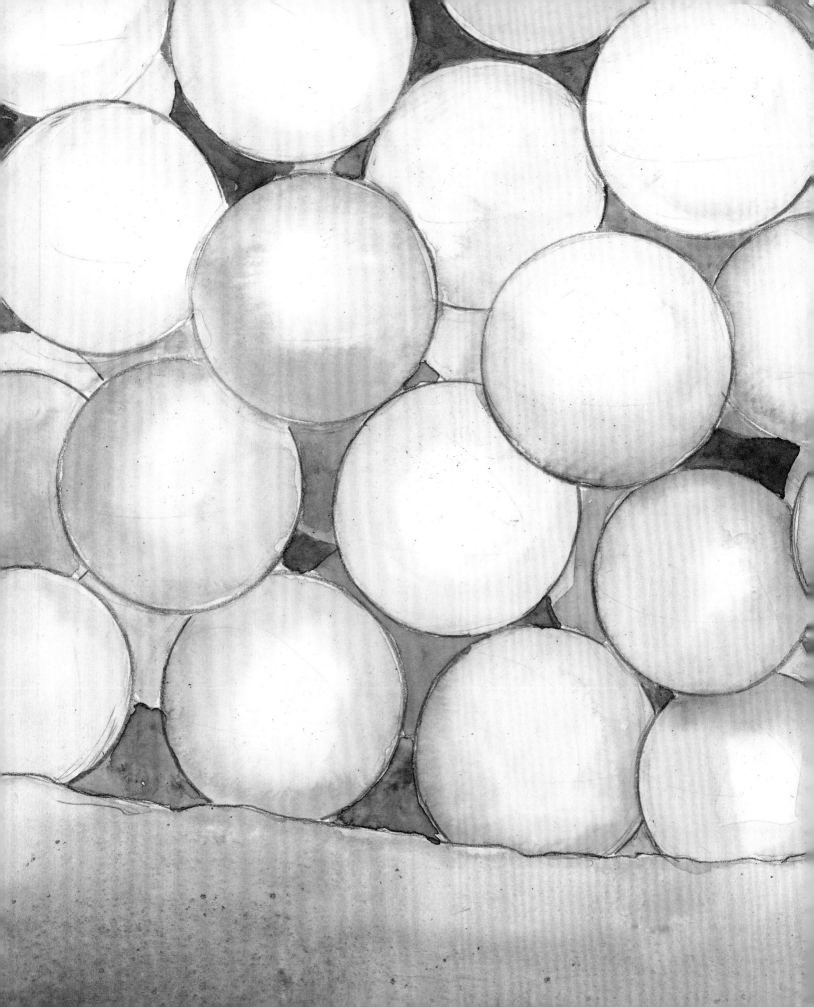

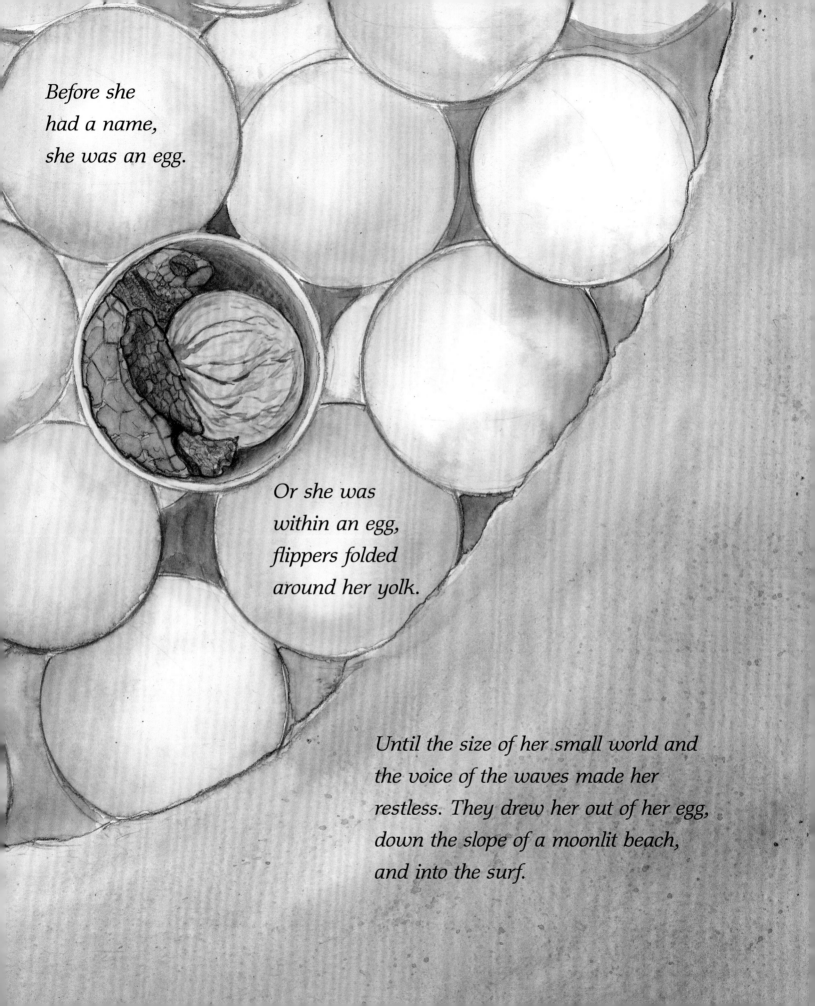

Before she
had a name,
she was an egg.

Or she was
within an egg,
flippers folded
around her yolk.

Until the size of her small world and
the voice of the waves made her
restless. They drew her out of her egg,
down the slope of a moonlit beach,
and into the surf.

FOR JULES AND REESA AND OF COURSE YOSHI

Yoshi and the Ocean: A Sea Turtle's Incredible Journey Home. Copyright © 2022 by Lindsay Moore. All rights reserved. Manufactured in Italy. For information address HarperCollins Children's Books, a division of HarperCollins Publishers, 195 Broadway, New York, NY 10007. www.harpercollinschildrens.com. The full-color art was rendered in graphite, watercolor, drawing inks, Conté crayon, and color pencils. The text type is 16-point Matt Antique. Library of Congress Cataloging-in-Publication Data. Names: Moore, Lindsay, author, illustrator. Title: Yoshi and the ocean : a sea turtle's incredible journey home / written and illustrated by Lindsay Moore. Description: First Edition. | New York : Greenwillow Books, an imprint of HarperCollins Publishers, [2022] | Audience: Ages 4–8 years | Audience: Grades 2–3 | Summary: "Yoshi, a loggerhead sea turtle, was injured and rescued by fishermen who took her to the Two Oceans Aquarium in South Africa for rehabilitation. After twenty years, Yoshi was returned to the sea and traveled nearly 23,000 miles over three years back to what is believed to be her birthplace"— Provided by publisher. Identifiers: LCCN 2021055293 | ISBN 9780063060982 (Hardcover). Subjects: LCSH: Loggerhead turtle—Anecdotes—Juvenile literature. | Turtles—Anecdotes—Juvenile literature. Classification: LCC QL795.T8 M66 2022 | DDC 597.92/89—dc23/eng/20220103 LC record available at https://lccn.loc.gov/2021055293 First Edition 23 24 25 26 RTLO 10 9 8 7 6 5 4 3 2 Greenwillow Books

LINDSAY MOORE

YOSHI AND THE OCEAN

A Sea Turtle's Incredible Journey Home

GREENWILLOW BOOKS
An Imprint of HarperCollinsPublishers

This is Yoshi, small and broken,

found by fishermen in the waves.

They give her a place to rest.
They give her fish to eat
from their nets,

and a name:

Yoshitaro.

This is Yoshi, little patient.

She is the first turtle the aquarium

in Cape Town has cared for.

They see the dent in her side.

They see the size of her spirit . . . and appetite.

They give her a home and time to heal.

"Yoshi"
Species: Loggerhead turtle
Origin: ?
Weight: 2kg
Length:

They learn how to feed her
and keep all their fingers.

She learns not to bite them
when she wants a snack.

They learn how to read
Yoshi's behavior.

She learns how to ask for
a scratch on the back.

Yoshi swims circles with silvery fish
and smooth stingrays.
She stops to watch the crowds
who watch with wonder.

Years begin and end and start again.
Visitors come and discover and go.
Yoshi swims at the aquarium
and eats and grows.

This is Yoshi, Queen of the Exhibit.

On the outside, she looks the same.

Inside, though, something has changed.

Now the walls of her world

make her restless.

She is from away from here,

and that is where she needs to go.

Those who care for her understand.

She is healthy now.

She should be in the ocean.

But they worry.

She has lived at the aquarium for twenty years.

Will she remember how to find food?

What about tiger sharks and ship strikes?

What about floating plastic and fishing snares?

They are not sure where she is from,

but they think it is where she will go.

They prepare her for a long journey.

She swims laps and eats more.

She is training to go home.

This is Yoshi, much-loved turtle.
Scientists glue a tracking tag
to her shell.

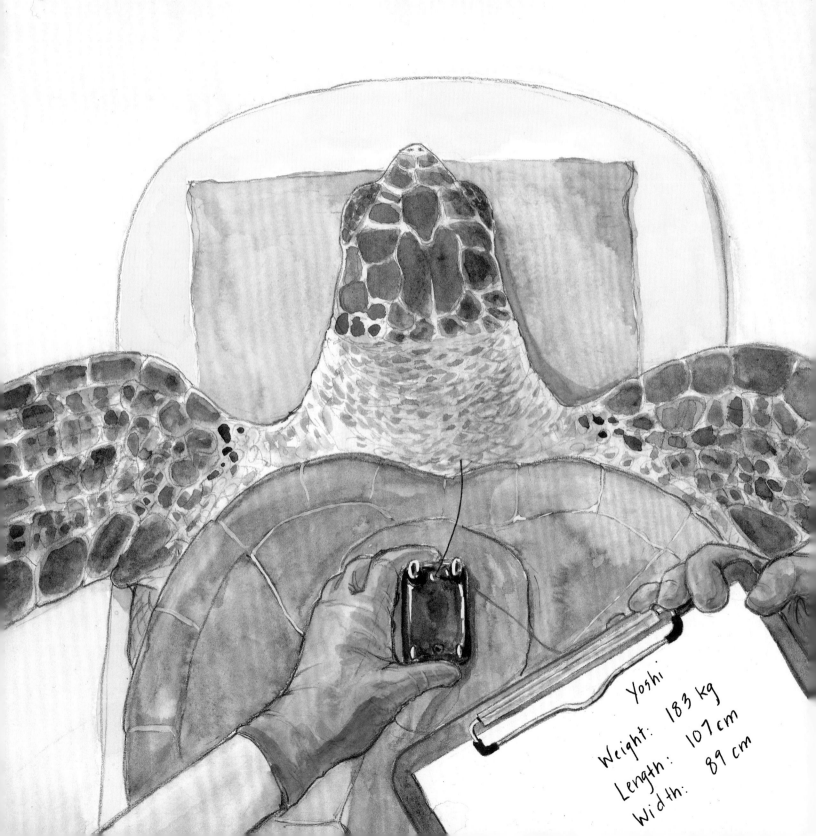

When the weather is calm and welcoming,

they take her out to deep water.

"Three . . . two . . . one . . .

go Yoshi!"

This is Yoshi, wild turtle.
She is remembering
what the ocean is like:
the shape of a wave,
the shift of the wind,
the push of a current . . .

and the sky.

Each time Yoshi stops at the surface for a breath of air,

a signal is sent out, strong and clear; to satellites

crisscrossing the exosphere.

Hello from Yoshi. I am here.

This is Yoshi, ocean wanderer.
She loops through plankton blooms
that form like clouds near the sunlit surface.
Miles of wispy gardens feed crowds of fish
and floating sea creatures.

A plankton bloom
attracts a feast
for pilchards and penguins
and Yoshi.

This is Yoshi, clever turtle.
On a single breath of air,
she dives down
below the blooms,
through scales and shells and fish guts
that fall like snow
on the oozing seabed.

Where the sun is not as strong,
she finds food for her journey.
Snails and clams, shrimp and crabs,
all make a delicious crunch.

This is Yoshi, intrepid turtle.

She winds her way northward, against warm currents,

against expectations.

"Where is she going?" they wonder in Cape Town.

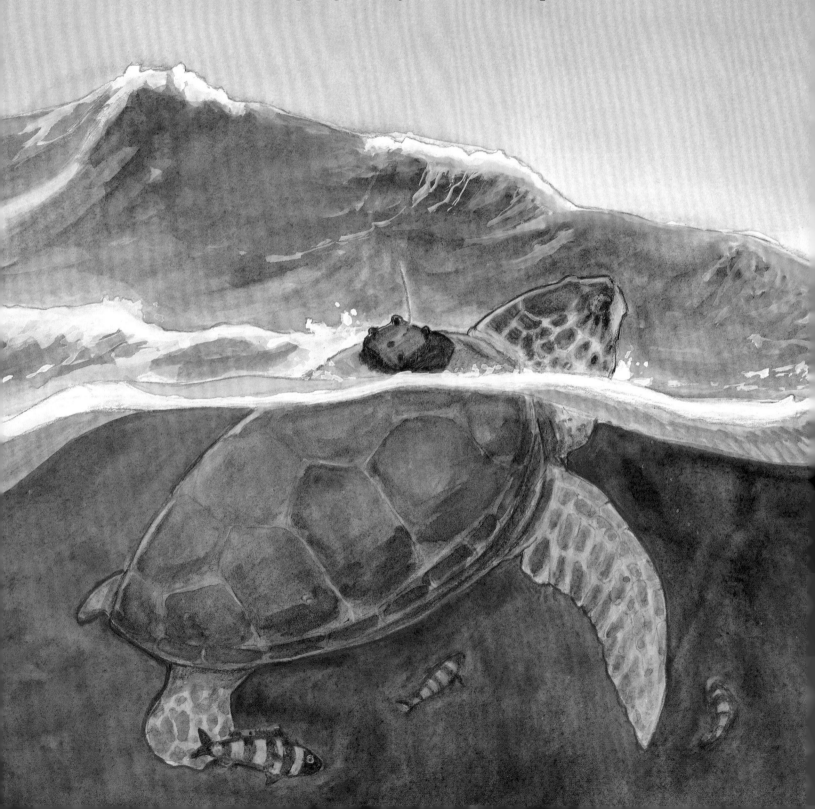

She swims north,
along the underwater edge of the African Continent,
sometimes right on the slope,
where the sea floor drops away into darkness,
the beginning of the abyss.

She swims in the space between two worlds—
the deep sea and the coastal sea.
Where worlds meet and water mixes, food is plentiful.
And so are fishing vessels.

She swims through busy fishing grounds,

where silent lines

hang easy snacks

from deadly hooks.

Those who love her, hold their breath.

Hello from Yoshi. I am here.

This is Yoshi, ocean turtle.
She crosses into the abyss
to swim among seamounts
that rise, miles high, off the ocean floor.
Rowdy currents roll up the steep sides.

There is plenty of food

for Yoshi to find

to fuel her on her journey.

She feasts for a while

then turns south,

and everyone wonders where she is going.

This is Yoshi, homeward-bound turtle.

She is rounding the cape where two oceans meet,

where currents collide.

Where waves are known to rise to like cliffs,

and swallow ships.

She swims east . . .
and everyone wonders
where she is going.

Hello from Yoshi.
I am here.

This is Yoshi, high-seas turtle.

She swims along underwater mountain ridges

that stretch like a seam across the ocean floor,

so deep

she cannot even reach their peaks.

There is less for her to stop and eat here,
but where warm water runs alongside cold,
food can be found.

Yoshi is not picky.

Her journey is wide like the wild.

It curves over the surface of the earth.

Eastward, eastward, across a deep ocean basin.

For weeks . . .

for months . . .

for a year.

Hello from Yoshi. I am here.

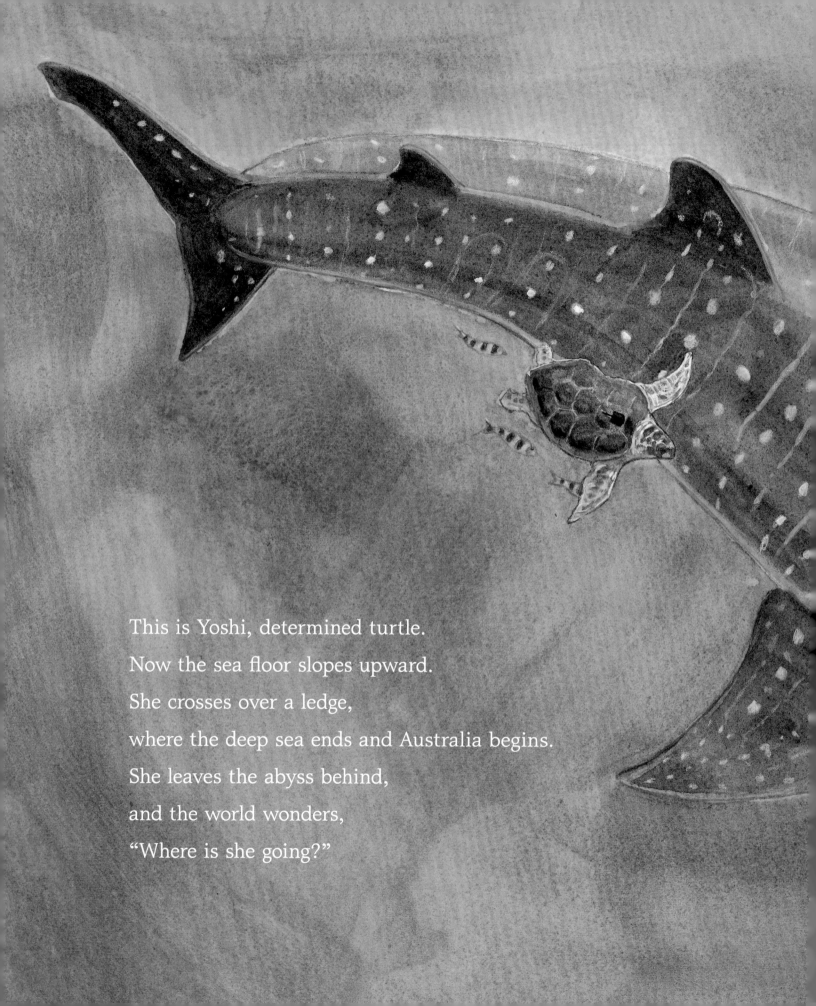

This is Yoshi, determined turtle.

Now the sea floor slopes upward.

She crosses over a ledge,

where the deep sea ends and Australia begins.

She leaves the abyss behind,

and the world wonders,

"Where is she going?"

She is going to where she belongs.

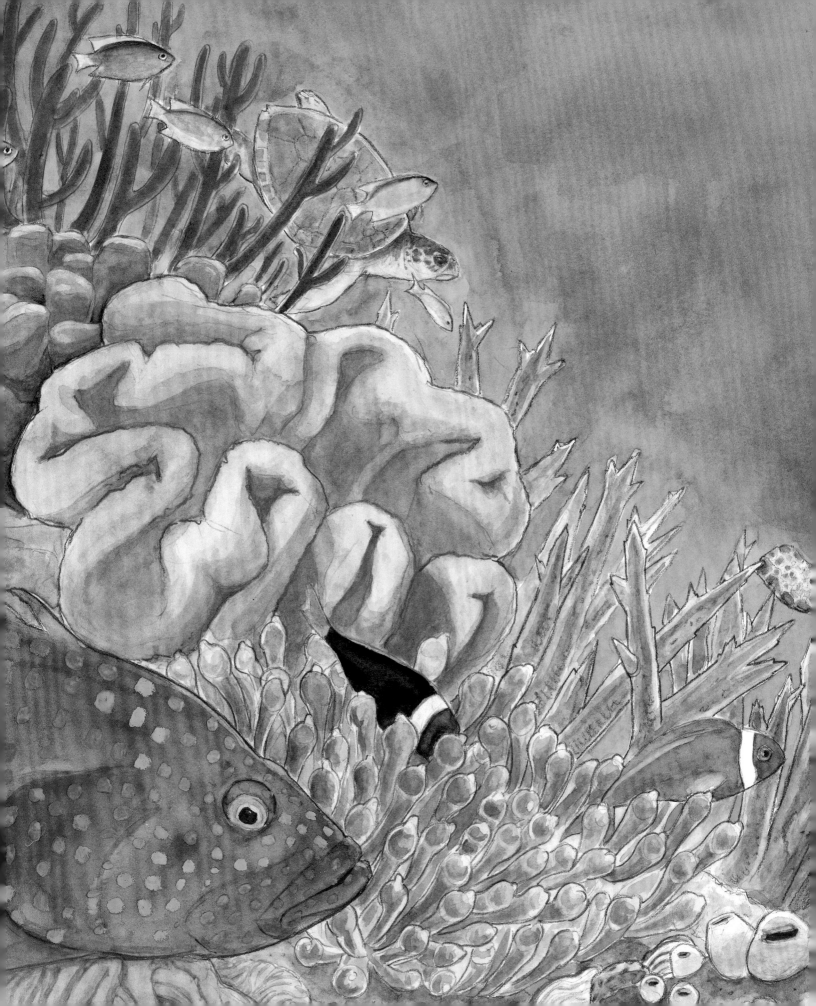

This is Yoshi, wild at heart.
She has left a life with walls and windows
and survived in untamed spaces.
She has crossed a wide ocean
to feed with other loggerheads in quiet places,
among mudflats, fields of seagrass,
and towering coral domes.

Hello from Yoshi.

I am home.

Yoshi's Journey

Yoshi was rescued by a Japanese fishing vessel in 1997 and brought to Two Oceans Aquarium in Cape Town, South Africa, to recover. Yoshi returned to the ocean on December 16, 2017, after living for twenty years in human care. Her 25,000-mile journey to reach Australian waters in February 2020 gives us insight into her mysterious origin. Female sea turtles return to the beach where they were born to lay eggs of their own, often swimming great distances to do so. Yoshi, like many released turtles, spent about a year swimming in loops. Then she picked up speed and headed straight across the Indian Ocean to reach Western Australia, where she stayed until her tracker stopped working, leading us to hope that she has finally found where she belongs.

1 Cape Town: Yoshi was released in the waters off Cape Town, South Africa.

10 Muiron Islands and Shark Bay: In Australia, loggerhead nesting season goes from December to March—the summer months—and peaks in January. It is believed that loggerheads foraging in the Pilbara and Kimberley regions return to Muiron Island, Dirk Hartog Island, and nearby coastal beaches to nest.

9 Eighty Mile Beach, Western Australia: Yoshi stays in the tropical waters of the Pilbara and Kimberley regions. Her satellite data leads researchers to a popular loggerhead feeding ground previously unknown to science. It is believed that loggerheads from these grounds nest in Western Australia. Yoshi's last transmission, from the waters off Eighty Mile Beach, was in October 2020.

8 Australian Continental Shelf: Continents extend underwater as continental shelves. There is plenty of food in the shallow, sunlit waters, so many animals make their home there.

Africa

Atlantic Ocean

Angola

Namibia

South Africa

2 Benguela Upwelling System: Along the southwest coast of Africa, deep currents carry nutrients up to the surface and fuel plankton blooms that attract many fish, birds, and marine mammals. There are also many commercial fishing boats in the area.

India

Indian Ocean

Pacific Ocean

3 African Continental Shelf: Yoshi spent time feasting over the continental shelf along the coasts of South Africa, Namibia, and Angola.

4 Walvis Ridge and Seamounts: Undersea mountains provide habitats and hunting grounds for many ocean animals, including sea turtles.

9

8

10

Australia

5 The Cape of Good Hope: While it is a ship graveyard famous for high winds and rogue waves, the mixing currents of the Atlantic and Indian Oceans and rising seamounts make it a place teeming with ocean life.

—— Yoshi's journey

Continental shelf: water less than 650 feet deep

Ocean basin: water greater than 650 feet deep

Land

⋀ Seamounts

—— Warm currents

—— Cold currents

Known nesting sites for loggerhead sea turtles of the Indian Ocean

7 Southwest Indian Ridge: A deep ocean ridge that stretches across the Indian Ocean basin.

6 Agulhas Current: In the open ocean, phytoplankton blooms can occur along current boundaries, where differences in temperature and salinity cause seawater to mix, bringing nutrients from the deep to the surface.

Loggerhead Sea Turtles, *Caretta caretta*

Loggerheads have bodies built for life in the ocean. Their streamlined shape and paddle-like limbs make them excellent swimmers. Their large size and hard, heavy shell, while difficult to manage on land, protect them from predators in the water. Like other reptiles, they breathe air, are covered with scales, are cold-blooded, and lay eggs. Sea turtles, along with sea snakes, marine iguanas, and some crocodiles, are one of the few reptiles uniquely adapted for life in the ocean.

Salt gland
Sea turtles have adapted to drink salt water. They excrete excess salt through tear glands located near their eyes.

Scales

Forelimb

Claws

Loggerhead Shells
Turtle shells are modified rib cages designed to provide structure and act as armor. They are made of bone and covered with special scales called scutes. Scutes are made of keratin, like our fingernails, and grow larger and thicker as the turtle matures.

Predators
When sea turtles are small, they have many different predators. Insects, foxes, crabs, sea birds, and fish (including sharks) all pose a threat to bite-sized turtles, before and after they hatch. But as a sea turtle grows and its shell strengthens, very few predators bother them. One common predator to adult loggerheads is the tiger shark, whose wide mouth and sharp teeth are well suited to hunting large prey.

Scutes
Loggerheads can be distinguished from other species of sea turtles by the number and pattern of their scutes.

Barnacles

Floating Habitats
Loggerhead turtles are often observed with barnacles, algae, and crabs living on their shells. Looking closer, scientists discovered a microscopic world where thousands (and sometimes hundreds of thousands) of water bears, mud dragons, nematodes, and other small animals, together known as meiofauna, thrive.

Hind limb
Female sea turtles use their hind limbs to dig out nests in the sand when they lay their eggs.

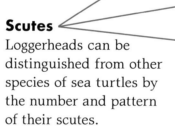

Water bear **Mud dragon** **Nematode**

Skull

Esophagus
Transports food from the mouth to the stomach.

Right lung
Loggerheads have two large lungs and can hold their breath to make dives up to 650 feet deep in search of food. Dive length depends on the size of the turtle and the water temperature, but turtles spend about ninety percent of their time underwater.

Loggerhead Esophagus
Eating in the ocean can be a challenge. The loggerhead esophagus is lined with keratinous spikes, so that ingested food is trapped moving inward along the digestive tract while sea water is expelled out of the turtle's mouth before swallowing.

Loggerhead   **Human**

This ancient design has become problematic in recent times because of the presence of plastic floating in the ocean. If a turtle swallows plastic, she cannot cough it back up because the spikes trap the plastic just like they trap food. The plastic must travel all the way through the turtle's digestive tract. It can slow digestion, make the turtle sick, and even lead to death.

Hidden hand
Inside each paddle-shaped forelimb are five fingers.

Loggerhead Life Cycle
Loggerhead sea turtles may live 80 years or more. A loggerhead turtle begins its life inside an egg about the size of a Ping-Pong ball.

A female turtle emerges from the ocean at night to dig a nest. She lays about 100 eggs, covers the nest, and returns to the ocean. The eggs incubate for 60-75 days before the hatchlings emerge.

• Female turtles lay eggs every two to three years. They may dig one to six nests in a season.

• At around 20 years old, female turtles are old enough to lay eggs of their own.

• Yoshi spent 20 years in the care of Two Oceans Aquarium.

• Relying on their instincts, hatchlings enter a period that lasts 24 hours called the "frenzy," where they rush to the waves, dodging predators on land and in the water to swim out into open ocean currents. Young turtles often travel thousands of miles as they ride in currents around ocean basins.

• After 10 years, they swim to more coastal waters and continue to eat and grow.

Eggs

60-75 days

Frenzy 24 hours

Open ocean stage

10 years

Yoshi's life at the aquarium

10 years

Juvenile coastal stage

Coastal adult stage

60 years

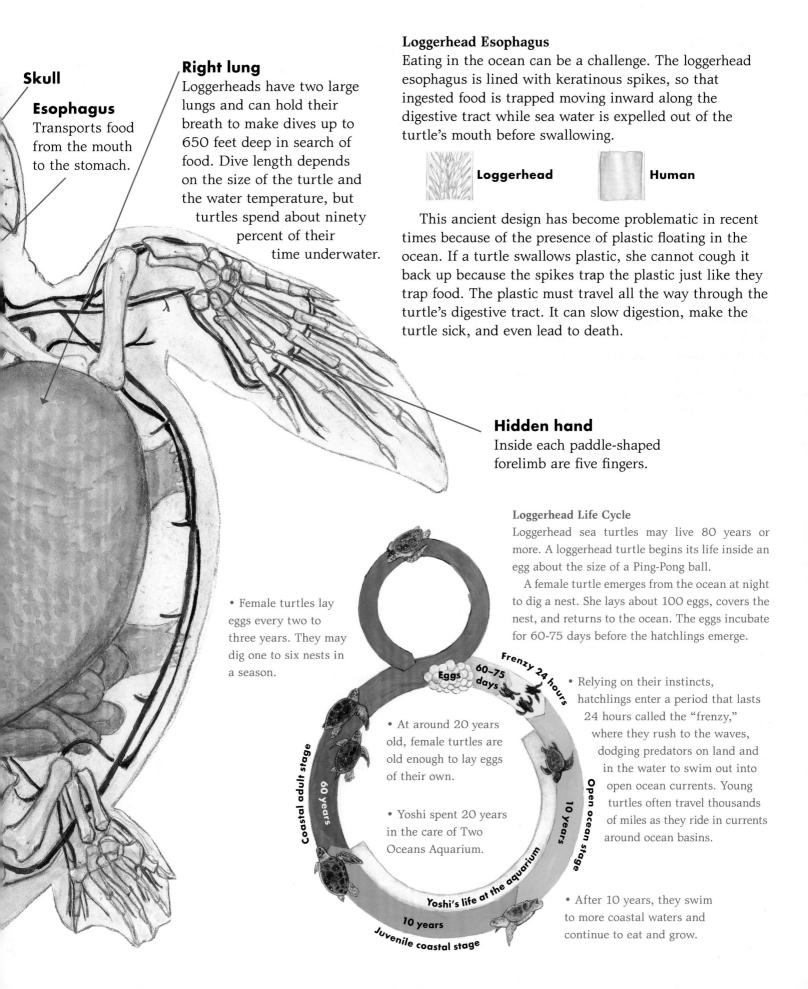

Finding Food in the Ocean

Just like on land, the base of the ocean's food web is plants, mostly microscopic floating algae known as phytoplankton. Phytoplankton, like all plants, need three things to bloom: water, sunlight, and nutrients. A phytoplankton bloom supports grazers, zooplankton (mostly microscopic invertebrates and larvae), and small fish. These in turn attract larger animals, carnivores that get most of their energy from eating meat.

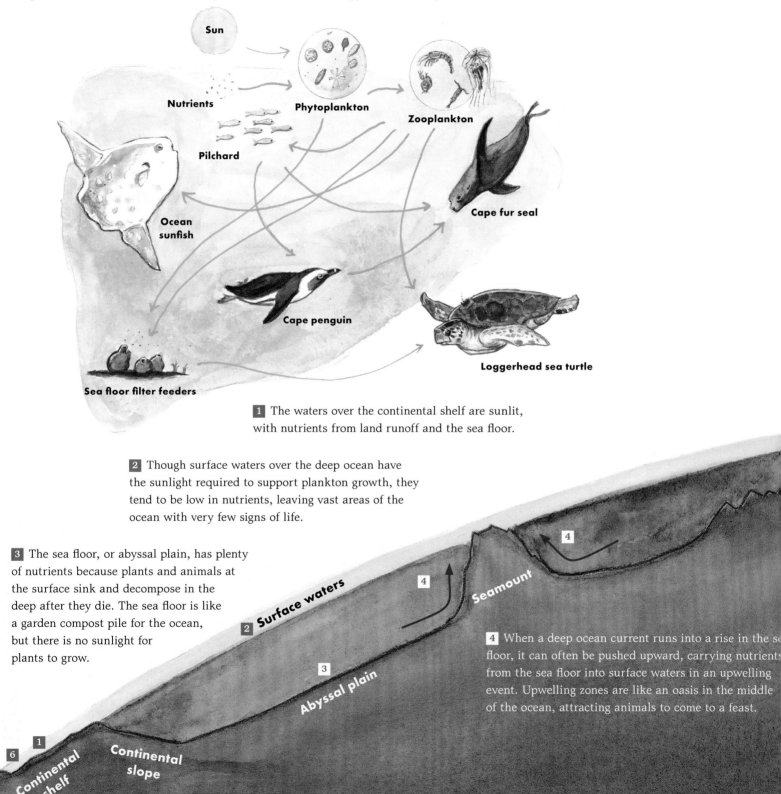

Sun

Nutrients

Phytoplankton

Zooplankton

Pilchard

Ocean sunfish

Cape fur seal

Cape penguin

Loggerhead sea turtle

Sea floor filter feeders

1 The waters over the continental shelf are sunlit, with nutrients from land runoff and the sea floor.

2 Though surface waters over the deep ocean have the sunlight required to support plankton growth, they tend to be low in nutrients, leaving vast areas of the ocean with very few signs of life.

3 The sea floor, or abyssal plain, has plenty of nutrients because plants and animals at the surface sink and decompose in the deep after they die. The sea floor is like a garden compost pile for the ocean, but there is no sunlight for plants to grow.

4 When a deep ocean current runs into a rise in the sea floor, it can often be pushed upward, carrying nutrients from the sea floor into surface waters in an upwelling event. Upwelling zones are like an oasis in the middle of the ocean, attracting animals to come to a feast.

Surface waters

Seamount

Abyssal plain

Continental shelf

Continental slope

Currents

Currents are like rivers flowing through the ocean. They move water and carry plants and animals, as well as oxygen and important nutrients, all around the globe. Surface currents are pushed by wind and the movement of the earth, while deeper currents flow because of differences in temperature and the amount of salt in the water. There are warm currents and cold currents, with different plants and animals found in each. Loggerhead hatchlings spend their first ten years riding along in warm currents.

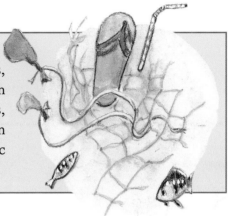

Plastics in the Ocean
Currents also consolidate trash, lost fishing gear, and plastics, collecting the floating debris in their flow. Plastics from land can be found far out at sea. Plastic debris is dangerous to animals, such as sea turtles, when they mistake it for food. Sea turtles can also become entangled while hunting for food hiding in plastic debris.

5 Ocean mixing can also occur in the open ocean at current fronts, areas where bodies of water with different temperatures and densities meet. Current fronts can extend for hundreds of feet to thousands of miles.

6 Adult loggerhead turtles prefer the shallow waters located over the continental shelf, where nutritious prey is easy to dive for.

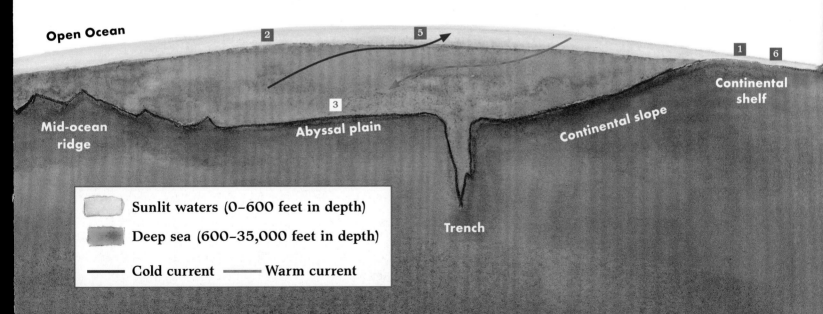

Open Ocean

2   5

1 6

Continental shelf

3

Continental slope

Mid-ocean ridge

Abyssal plain

Trench

☐ Sunlit waters (0–600 feet in depth)

☐ Deep sea (600–35,000 feet in depth)

—— Cold current   —— Warm current

The Ocean Floor
There are hills, mountains, plains, valleys, canyons, and even volcanoes in the ocean. And just as you might find a frog in a pond or a squirrel in a tree, animals in the ocean have specific habitats as well. Most of the ocean animals we think of live along the continental shelf or the coast, where there is plenty of food and places to grow on or hide in. By comparison, the open ocean can seem like a desert, endlessly blue with few signs of life. Seamounts and ocean ridges attract long-distance ocean travelers, like Yoshi. They are habitat for a diverse population of plants and animals. The currents surrounding them provide nutrients to support life.

SEA TURTLES today navigate oceans filled with many man-made hazards. Turtles can be accidentally caught in fishing gear as bycatch. They can ingest plastic or become entangled. They face habitat loss from both coastal development and sea level rise due to climate change. They can be confused by light pollution near nesting beaches. Yet all around the world, people are working to protect sea turtles in big and small ways, through beach cleanups, public education, the legislation and creation of Marine Protected Areas, dark-sky programs, sea turtle rescue and rehabilitation efforts, research, and improving fishing techniques to reduce bycatch. Kids are pledging to use less plastic, using less energy by turning off lights and screens, organizing beach or neighborhood cleanups (even if you do not live near the ocean, local litter can still end up there), and educating others and writing their government officials about sustainability.

For more information about sea turtles and what you can do to help them, visit:

National Oceanic and Atmospheric Administration (NOAA):
www.fisheries.noaa.gov/feature-story/what-can-you-do-save-sea-turtles

North Carolina Aquarium at Fort Fisher:
www.seaturtleexploration.com/

National Geographic Kids:
www.kids.nationalgeographic.com/
animals/reptiles/facts/loggerhead-sea-turtle

Sea Turtle Conservancy:
www.conserveturtles.org/educational-initiatives-educator-resources/

The State of the World's Sea Turtles (SWOT):
www.seaturtlestatus.org/how-you-can-help

Photo: Two Oceans Aquarium

Yoshi and a diver at Two Oceans Aquarium.

For more information about Yoshi's journey:
The Two Oceans Aquarium blog (www.aquarium.co.za/blog) features many posts about sea turtles and other ocean animals. The October 28, 2020, blog entry includes a roundup of news about Yoshi as well as some amazing photographs.

Bibliography and Resources
Research for this book was extensive and wide-ranging, and the following primarily scholarly resources were the most helpful to me:

Barale, Vittorio, Martin Gade. *Remote Sensing of the African Seas*. Dordrecht: Springer, 2014.
Bolten, Alan, Blair Witherington. *Loggerhead Sea Turtles*. Washington: Smithsonian Books, 2003.

Carr, Archie. *Handbook of Turtles: The Turtles of the United States, Canada, and Baja California*. Ithaca: Cornell University Press, 1952.
Wyneken, Jeanette. *The Anatomy of Sea Turtles*, Miami: U.S. Department of Commerce NOAA Technical Memorandum NMFS-SEFSC-470, 2001.
Wyneken, Jeanette, Kenneth J. Lohmann, John A. Musick. *The Biology of Sea Turtles, Volume III*. Boca Raton: CRC Press, 2013.

Acknowledgments
Thank you to Maryke Musson and the staff of Two Oceans Aquarium for chronicling Yoshi's journey, and for the work they do in sea turtle rehabilitation and marine environmental education. Without their work, this book would not have been written. I would also like to thank conservation biologist Dr. Anne Savage—who has spent countless hours studying sea turtles in Florida and around the world—for reviewing the text and art with a thoughtful eye, and for sharing important resources to make this story stronger. Thank you also to Dr. Scott Whiting, principal scientist with the Western Australia Department of Biodiversity, Conservation and Attractions, for sharing his expertise on sea turtles in Australian waters. A sincere thank-you as well to Dr. Joseph Warren, professor at Stony Brook University, for answering questions and reviewing the information on oceanography for this book. A special thank-you to the Davis clan—Joel, Amity, and Lachlan—who have supported me through this project, and to Virginia Duncan, who first shared Yoshi's story with me.

Staying in Touch

Scientists often place tracking devices on animals in the wild to learn about their behavior. The scientists at the aquarium glued a tag on Yoshi's shell before they released her. The tag, which doesn't hurt, had an antenna on it that was programmed to transmit information about Yoshi's location to satellites orbiting Earth when Yoshi came up to the surface to breathe. The information from the satellite was then transmitted to the scientists who shared Yoshi's progress with the world. Yoshi sent 23,167 satellite messages during her incredible journey.

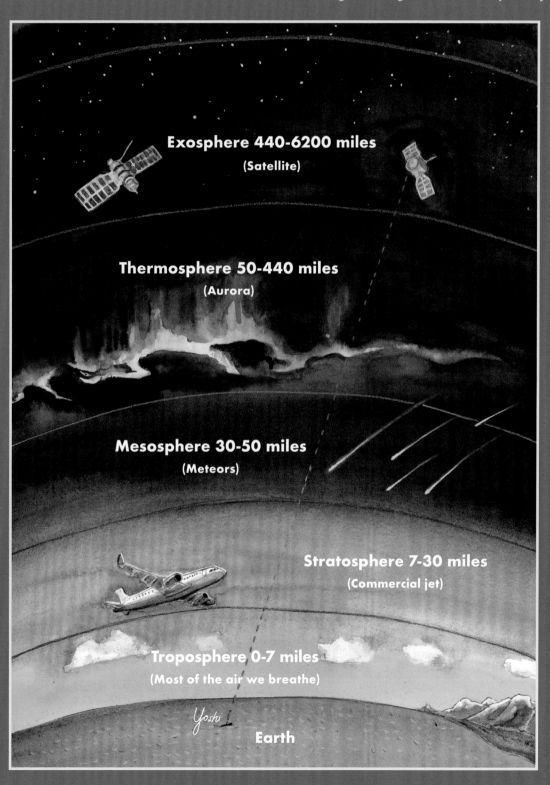